The Military History of World War I

1914: THE BATTLES
IN THE WEST

by Trevor Nevitt Dupuy,
COL., U.S. ARMY, RET.

FRANKLIN WATTS, INC.
575 Lexington Avenue • New York, N.Y. 10022

Author and publisher wish to thank the following copyright holders for permission to include the maps listed below:

The maps on pages 6–7, 28, and 55 are reproduced with the permission of McGraw-Hill Book Company from *Military Heritage of America*, by Dupuy and Dupuy.

The map on page 52 is reproduced with the permission of Charles Scribner's Sons from *Military History of The World War*, page 72, by Girard L. McEntee. Copyright 1937 Charles Scribner's Sons; renewal copyright © 1965 Helen S. McEntee and Girard L. McEntee.

The map on page 68 is reproduced with the permission of Frederick A. Praeger, Inc. from *A Concise History of World War I*, Prepared for *The Encyclopedia Americana* under the Advisory Editorship of Brigadier General Vincent J. Esposito, USA (Ret.), Frederick A. Praeger, Inc., Publishers, New York, 1964.

The maps on pages 78 and 84 are reproduced with the permission of Houghton Mifflin Company and Thomas Nelson & Sons, Ltd., London, from *History of the Great War*, by John Buchan.

1. European War, 1914-1918.

Contents

The Military History of World War I

1914: THE BATTLES
IN THE WEST

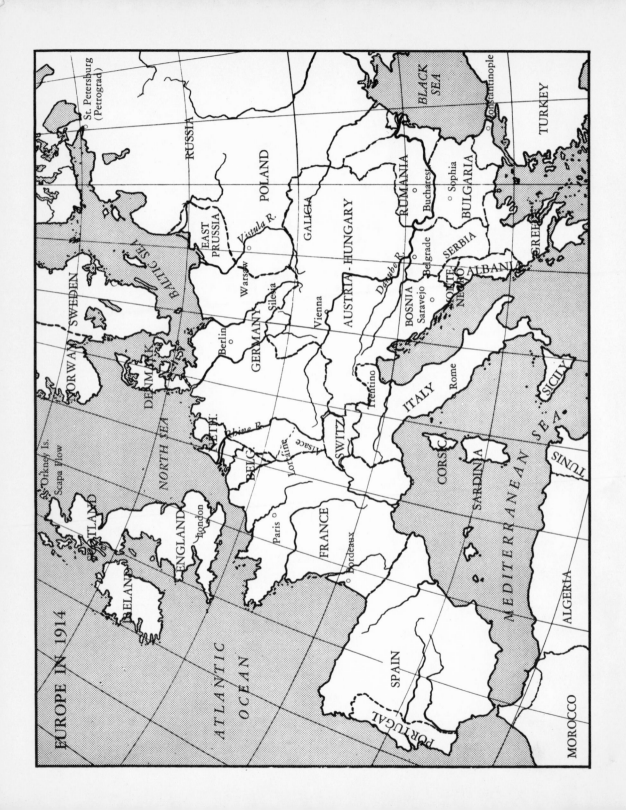

EUROPE IN 1914

Alliance vs Entente

Legacy of the Franco-Prussian War

The Franco-Prussian War of 1870–71 left the German Empire the strongest power on continental Europe. Together with the complete humiliation of France, Germany obtained the French province of Alsace and part of Lorraine. The swiftness of the German victory had alarmed other countries in Europe and created an atmosphere that eventually led to World War I more than forty years later.

For France, the period from 1871 to 1914 was one of hatred of Germany. Although she was militarily beaten in 1870, and forced to pay a large indemnity to Germany, the natural wealth of France, her colonial empire, and her basic national unity enabled her to recover quickly. By 1914 France was second only to Germany among the powers on the continent of Europe. French desire to regain Alsace-Lorraine made it seem that a war of revenge was inevitable.

During this same period, Germany was consolidating her continental empire and expanding her industry at home and trade abroad. As a commercial and industrial nation, she was exceeded only by Great Britain, but her need for markets and raw materials created a desire for a colonial empire. Both Great Britain and France had numerous colonies, but Germany started her colonial search later. Thus she was forced to obtain her colonies in remote and less desirable regions — in southern Africa, bits of Asia, and the South Pacific. In order to maintain and protect this colonial system a fleet was necessary, so, at the end of the nineteenth century, Germany started to

1

build a large navy. This naturally aroused the suspicions and hostility of Great Britain who, as an island empire, wished to remain the supreme naval power.

Conflicts of Interest in Eastern Europe

During the late nineteenth and early twentieth centuries, the Austro-Hungarian Empire was slowly decaying. However, the Austrians had hopes of increasing their strength and territory in the Balkans at the expense of the even more decadent Ottoman Turkish Empire. The Hapsburg monarchy in Austria-Hungary was plagued with continuing internal unrest, caused by friction between the Germanic, Magyar, and Slavic peoples within the empire. This friction was increased by the desire of many of the Slavic peoples of the southern provinces to join neighboring Serbia. In addition, the ambitions of Austria-Hungary in the Balkans had antagonized Russia, which also had vital interests in this area.

The Russian Empire, although the largest nation in Europe, was in some ways even weaker than Austria-Hungary. Having been badly beaten in the Russo-Japanese War of 1904–5, Russia was also weakened by internal revolutionary unrest. She was having difficulty in changing from an agrarian to an industrial economy, and in consolidating internal groups as diverse as those of Austria-Hungary. Nevertheless, Russia entertained ideas of expansion in the Balkans to gain an access to the Mediterranean Sea. This resulted in a conflict of interests with Austria-Hungary. It also caused the Austrians to believe that Russia was responsible for stirring up unrest among the Slavs in the Balkans.

2

The Alliances

These conflicting national interests in Western and Eastern Europe caused the major European powers to group themselves into protective alliance systems. The first steps were taken after the Franco-Prussian War by Germany's chancellor, Otto von Bismarck, who tried to preserve peace in Europe while strengthening the new German Empire. He soon realized that the friction between Russia and Austria-Hungary made it impossible for Germany to keep the friendship of both countries. So, in 1878, he concluded a defensive alliance with Austria-Hungary against Russia. Three years later Italy joined, to create the Triple Alliance. Germany and Austria agreed they would support Italy, if she were attacked by France, in exchange for Italian agreement to stay neutral in case of war between Austria-Hungary and Russia.

Bismarck also realized the possibility of an alliance between France and Russia against Germany (which actually occurred in 1893). To balance this, he attempted to maintain friendly relations with Britain. In 1890, however, young Kaiser Wilhelm II dismissed Bismarck from the chancellorship and soon aroused British suspicions by building up the German navy and creating a colonial empire in Africa and the Pacific. This led to an Anglo-French alliance in 1904, confirming Bismarck's earlier fears. By supporting Austrian ambitions in the Balkans, Wilhelm also embittered Russia, and this in turn led to an Anglo-Russian alliance. In 1907 these two alliances were joined in the Triple Entente — an alliance between Great Britain, France, and Russia.

The Triple Entente, offset by the Triple Alliance, divided Europe into two armed camps. In addition, several other lesser countries were involved indirectly in these alliances. Great Britain, France, and Germany had jointly guaranteed Belgian neutrality. Also, in order to prevent further Austrian expansion into the Balkans, and out of sympathy with her "little Slavic sister," Russia practically guaranteed aid to Serbia in case of an Austro-Hungarian attack.

The Military Staffs

While European diplomats were busy concluding these alliances, there was comparable activity among military men. The primary reason for France's crushing defeat in 1870–71 was recognized to be the superiority of the German General Staff. Consequently, during the next forty years, all the powers attempted to develop efficient staff systems.

The German Army General Staff was the most select, and most highly trained in all Europe. The German solution to problems of military coordination was to place the burden on a minimum number of carefully selected, highly trained staff officers. This already-efficient staff was steadily improved in the years after the Franco-Prussian War.

The French developed an organization of four staff sections under a chief of staff, which was to become the model for the United States Army. The British had two principal staff sections under a chief of staff. The other major European countries imitated the systems of either Germany or France. The Austrian staff system was a poor copy of the German; the Russian system an even poorer copy of the French.

Another major factor in the defeat of France in 1870 had been lack of a well-prepared French war plan. Recognizing this fact, all of the

European general staffs began developing war and mobilization plans designed to meet all possible combinations of opponents. The best known of these was the German Schlieffen Plan.

The Schlieffen Plan

In 1893, two years after Count Alfred von Schlieffen became Chief of the German Army General Staff, France and Russia signed their alliance. Schlieffen was aware of the dangers of fighting a major war on two fronts, and he recognized that France was the greater immediate threat. So he developed a strategic plan to defeat France quickly before Russia could mobilize and become a greater danger.

An attack through the difficult terrain and strong fortifications in the Alsace-Lorraine sector of the French border would be slow and costly, while an envelopment through the Swiss Alps was practically impossible. Schlieffen therefore decided to send a large enveloping force through southern Holland and Belgium. This attack would have the advantages of breaking through the weakly held Franco-Belgian border, and of surprising the French, who would not expect an attack through neutral Belgium and Holland.

Schlieffen planned to have the German right wing, pivoting on Metz, about seven times as strong as the left wing, which was to hold a defensive line from Metz to the Swiss border. Schlieffen rightly assumed that in war France would attack against the weaker German left wing in an attempt to regain Alsace and Lorraine, but he believed the combination of rugged terrain and German fortifications could stop any French attack without giving up much German territory. Schlieffen in fact wanted to induce the French to make such an

CENTRAL EUROPE
ARMY CONCENTRATIONS
AND OPPOSING PLANS
July 1914

0   50   100
Scale of miles

JUTLAND

DENMARK

Kiel Canal

Kiel

NORTH

SEA

Helgoland

Hamburg

UNITED KINGDOM

London

Amsterdam

NETHERLANDS

Meuse

Dover   Dunkirk
Calais

Antwerp

Scheldt R.

BELGIUM

Brussels

Namur   Liege   Cologne

Six ersatz corps to follow & relieve right wing of rear area duties

Dieppe

Somme R.

Le Havre

Amiens   Maubeuge

Rouen

Seine R.

Sedan   LUX   Coblenz

Paris

Reims   Verdun   Mainz

Marne R.

Orleans   Toul   Metz

Tours   *Loire R.*   Epinal

PLAN XVII

Note: Alternate employment of French 4th and 5th Armies in event Germans violated Belgian neutrality.

Belfort

Berne

SWITZERLAND   TYROL

AU

Rhone R.

Rhine R.

Moselle R.

Lyons

Trent

Milan

Turin   *Po R.*

ITALY   Venice

Genoa

Nice

FRANCE

GERMAN FORCES IN THE WEST

Schleiffen Plan-1905	1914 Modification
Right Flank	
90% of Mobile Forces Over 7 times as strong as Left Flank. To drive thru Holland & Belgium.	60% of Mobile Forces 3 times as strong as Left Flank. To drive thru Belgium, not Holland.
Left Flank	
5% of Mobile Forces To delay, withrawing slowly in front of expected French attack.	25% of Mobile Forces To repulse expected French attack, & drive back into France.

Circled army numbers on map: 1, 2, 3, 4, 5 (German); 5, 4, 3, 2, 1 (French); 6, 7

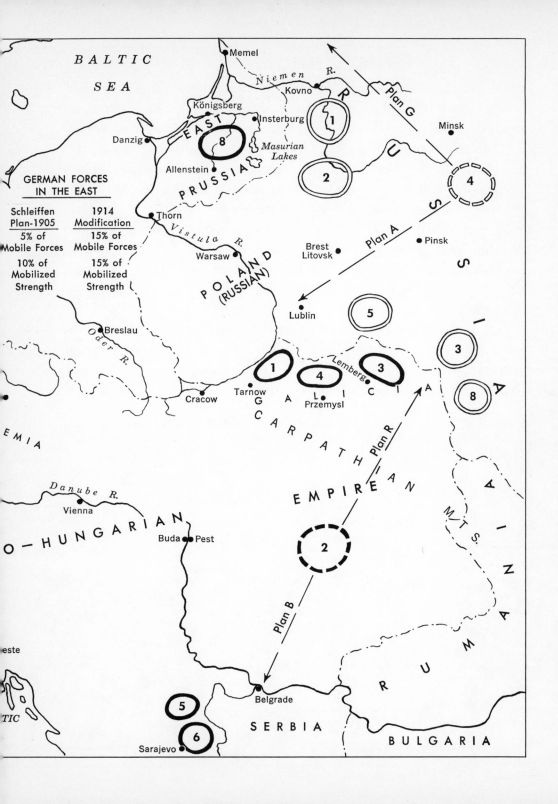

BALTIC
SEA

Memel

Niemen R.

Kovno

Plan G

Königsberg

Insterburg

Minsk

Danzig

EAST

8

Masurian
Lakes

1

Allenstein

PRUSSIA

2

4

Thorn

Vistula R.

R

U

S

S

I

A

GERMAN FORCES
IN THE EAST

Schleiffen
Plan–1905
5% of
Mobile Forces

1914
Modification
15% of
Mobile Forces

10% of
Mobilized
Strength

15% of
Mobilized
Strength

Warsaw

POLAND
(RUSSIAN)

Brest
Litovsk

Plan A

Pinsk

Oder R.

Breslau

Lublin

5

3

Cracow

Tarnow

1

4

Lemberg

3

8

Przemysl

G   A   L   I   C   I   A

CARPATHIAN

EMIA

Danube R.

Vienna

O – H U N G A R I A N

Buda

Pest

EMPIRE

Plan R

M

T

S

.

A

I

N

2

Plan B

U

M

R

este

TIC

5

6

Belgrade

SERBIA

R   U   M   A   N   I   A

BULGARIA

Sarajevo

attack on the German left, so that his sweeping right wing could swing behind the attacking French armies, which would then be crushed in a double envelopment between the two German wings.

On the Eastern Front a small German force was to hold against the slowly mobilizing Russians until Germany defeated France. Then Schlieffen's armies would be transferred to the East to defeat Russia.

After Schlieffen retired in 1905, he was succeeded by General Helmuth von Moltke, nephew of Field Marshal von Moltke of Franco-Prussian War fame. The younger Moltke was a different type of individual, and was faced with a changed situation by 1914. Although he still used the basic Schlieffen Plan, he modified it considerably to meet the new conditions.

Part of the new situation was that the Russian army, under pressure from France, could probably mobilize faster than Schlieffen had expected. Moltke believed this would require more troops to protect German East Prussia than Schlieffen had planned. Also, Moltke did

Kaiser Wilhelm II (left) with his six sons leads a military parade in Berlin.

General Helmuth von Moltke, Chief of the German Army General Staff, 1905– 14. (U.S. Signal Corps)

not want to give up any Prussian territory, as Schlieffen had believed might be temporarily necessary.

On the Western Front, Moltke decided to make the left wing stronger than originally planned. This was partly because of his general desire not to give up any German territory, and partly because he thought that the important German Rhineland industrial area needed better protection. He also decided not to attack through southern Holland, perhaps believing Great Britain might not enter the war to defend Belgium if Holland were spared.

As a result of these changes, the German West Front right wing was only four times as strong as the left wing, instead of being seven times stronger, as Schlieffen had planned. Another disadvantage of these changes was that the two rightmost German armies would have to be funneled through the fortified bottleneck of Liège in Belgium.

French Plan XVII

In 1911 the French Commander in Chief, General Victor Michel, anticipated the Schlieffen Plan, and prepared a plan to attack through Belgium as soon as the Germans violated that country's neutrality. This meant reducing French strength along her eastern frontier, which was opposed by many in the government. They also feared that this plan might lead France to violate Belgium's neutrality accidentally, and thus might keep Britain from entering the war on the French side. Above all, since it meant abandonment of an immediate attack to recover Alsace-Lorraine, Michel's plan was not accepted, and he was replaced as commander in chief by General Joseph Joffre.

General Joseph Joffre, Commander in Chief of the French army, 1911–17, in full-dress uniform before the outbreak of World War I. (U.S. Signal Corps)

Between 1911 and 1914 Joffre developed a new war plan, called Plan XVII. It called for the French armies to concentrate along the border from Switzerland to Belgium and in event of war to attack and regain Alsace and Lorraine. Although Joffre realized that Germany might violate Belgium's neutrality, he believed that the German armies could not go west of the Meuse without becoming overextended. Informal planning with the British resulted in an arrangement whereby the British Expeditionary Force would occupy a position on the French left flank in the event of a general European war.

The primary weakness of Plan XVII was the fact that French intelligence sources did not discover the efficient state of training of the German reserves, which would allow the German army to have a greater initial first-line strength than the French expected. This actually gave the Germans a substantial numerical superiority over the French, and permitted a wider sweep to the west than Joffre had believed possible.

11

The French war plan relied upon a doctrine of constant offensive. French military theorists believed that a determined attacker could fight his way through any defenses. They were convinced that victory in battle would come to the side with the ability and willpower to continue to attack under the most difficult circumstances. Also, they believed that the spirit of French soldiers was particularly suited to this doctrine of "offensive to the utmost." Because of their certainty that this doctrine was bound to bring victory, and to keep French troops from even thinking about defensive fighting, French leaders conducted little training in defense.

The Germans had an offensive doctrine almost as aggressive as the French. But the German Army General Staff recognized that there would be times when defensive fighting would be necessary. Thus German troops were trained in defense, and they were equipped with a greater number of machine guns for defensive fighting.

Other European War Plans

In the East, the war plans of both Russia and Austria-Hungary were shaped to conform to the German intentions. Russia had a defensive plan to be used if Germany should attack Russia first. Upon French insistence, the Russians also had a plan for an early invasion of East Prussia if, as the French General Staff expected, Germany first attacked France.

Austria-Hungary also had two plans. One was for a war in the Balkans, with Serbia as the probable enemy. The other plan was for war against both Russia and Russia's ally, Serbia. In the latter case the Austrians expected to be fighting alongside their German partners of the Triple Alliance, and they agreed to an early attack into Russian Poland to discourage the possibility of a Russian invasion of lightly defended East Prussia.

There were three other important participants in the early operations of the war, and each of these had war plans. Britain concentrated her attention on being prepared to meet the German challenge in a war at sea. As we have seen, the British land-war plan was to fit her small, but excellent, regular army into the details of French Plan XVII.

The war plans of Belgium and Serbia — both small nations — were very similar. They planned to defend their frontiers against invasion as long as they could, in hopes that larger-scale operations on the other fronts between the major contestants would relieve the pressure on their embattled forces before they were overwhelmed.

Thus the countries of Europe had spent over forty years since 1870 in preparation for a war many felt must surely come. In this atmosphere of friction and hostility which existed among the powers, all that was needed was a spark to set the entire Continent afire.

It was because of this atmosphere that politicians and military men of all nations felt that war was probably inevitable. At the same time, all were convinced that the power of new weapons, and the terrible expense of mobilizing, moving, and directing millions of men employing such weapons, would make the cost of war unbearable both physically and financially. Thus all authorities agreed that when the war came, it would be mercifully short.

Archduke Franz Ferdinand, and his wife, Duchess Sophie, at Sarajevo, June 28, 1914, in the automobile in which they were shot to death a few minutes after this photograph was taken. (United Press International)

"The Lamps Go Out"

Sarajevo

On June 28, 1914, the Archduke Franz Ferdinand of Austria-Hungary, accompanied by his wife, arrived at Sarajevo, the capital of Bosnia. This was a province Austria had annexed six years earlier from Turkey, after a long and complicated international dispute. Serbia had been particularly unhappy about the annexation, since a majority of the people of Bosnia were Serbians. Ferdinand was heir to the crown of the Austro-Hungarian Empire.

During passage of the motorcade celebrating his arrival, both the Archduke and his wife were assassinated by a Serbian terrorist,

Gavrilo Princip. In the investigation that followed, it was discovered that Princip was a member of a Serbian nationalistic secret society. It also came to light that Princip had plotted the assassination in Serbia.

To the Austro-Hungarian government, the assassination was proof of Serbian hostility. It also supplied an excuse to take action against Serbia. Field Marshal Franz Conrad von Hötzendorf, chief of the Austrian General Staff, had long urged war against Serbia. He was now supported by the Austrian Foreign Minister, Count Leopold von Berchtold. Prior to taking any warlike steps, however, it was necessary to determine what action Germany would take in support of Austria: specifically whether or not Germany would protect Austria-Hungary from an attack in the rear by Russia.

At an audience with Wilhelm II on July 5, the Austrian ambassador to Germany was assured by the Kaiser that Germany would support any action taken by Austria-Hungary to obtain satisfaction from Serbia. Wilhelm informed Theobald von Bethmann-Hollweg, the German Chancellor (Prime Minister), and General Erich von Falkenhayn, the Minister of War, of his decision, and then left for a vacation cruise near Norway.

On July 7, Berchtold and the Austrian Cabinet agreed to present a humiliating ultimatum to Serbia. This was so worded that it could not be accepted without a virtual renunciation of Serbian sovereignty. At this time, however, French President Raymond Poincaré and Prime Minister René R. Viviani were visiting Russia. Berchtold delayed delivery of the ultimatum to Serbia since he did not want it to arrive in Belgrade while the French leaders were consulting with their Russian allies.

The ultimatum, with a forty-eight-hour deadline for reply, was presented to Serbia on the evening of July 23. By the next afternoon

15

Kaiser Wilhelm II of Germany. (Imperial War Museum)

all Europe knew of its terms. The Russian government, although furious about the ultimatum, advised Serbia to accept as much of it as possible. Following Russian advice, Serbia made a conciliatory reply. At the same time Russia delivered a stern warning to Austria-Hungary.

Berchtold and Conrad, however, with assurance of German support, had never intended to accept Serbia's reply, no matter how conciliatory. But Emperor Franz Joseph, eighty-four years old and unaware of the intentions of his military and diplomatic advisers, was not entirely in favor of war after Serbia had accepted most of the Austrian demands. When Berchtold, on the twenty-sixth, asked for the Emperor's signature to the declaration of war, he also led Franz Joseph to believe that the Serbians had already fired on Austrian troops. Franz Joseph signed and Austria, which had mo-

16

Emperor Franz Joseph of Austria-Hungary. (Imperial War Museum)

bilized against Serbia on July 25, was ready to go to war.

The Kaiser returned to Berlin from his cruise on the twenty-sixth, but for reasons still not clear he did not see Serbia's reply until the morning of July 28. Upon reading the reply and seeing that Serbia had accepted most of the Austrian ultimatum, Wilhelm assumed that the threat of war had passed. At about that same time in Vienna, Berchtold was informing the Serbian ambassador that the reply was unacceptable and that a state of war existed.

During this period, Sir Edward Grey, the Foreign Secretary of Great Britain, proposed a conference of the powers to relieve tensions. He also suggested that the Kaiser mediate the dispute between Russia and Austria-Hungary. But the Austrians made clear their determination to punish Serbia. And the Austrian mobilization alarmed the Russians, who began to worry about the possibility of an Austrian attack.

Mobilization

The British fleet, due largely to the foresight of the First Lord of the Admiralty, Winston Churchill, had been assembled for a practice mobilization during the critical events of the summer. On the morning of July 29 the fleet sailed for its war stations at Scapa Flow. That evening the Czar ordered partial mobilization of the Russian army as a precaution against Austrian action.

It is difficult today to understand the effect that mobilization of a nation's armed forces had in 1914; most people assume that peace should always be possible up until either actual shooting or a declaration of war takes place. In 1914, however, with the existing tensions and fears, mobilization by one power had far-reaching effects. A nation could not allow a neighboring country to mobilize without mobilizing itself in order to be ready to protect itself. Nor could a nation control mobilization in the way that a water faucet can be turned on or off. In accordance with the established national war plan, there were detailed arrangements for concentration of troops at locations where weapons and equipment were stored. Train schedules were calculated and coordinated in precise detail. To attempt to alter or stop a mobilization once started would have created such confusion that the country's defensive position would have been worse than it was prior to mobilization. Since all the European powers understood these facts, it is not surprising that it was generally believed that mobilization by any one of the Great Powers would inevitably lead to war.

Declarations of War

Although Germany had not been responsible for starting the crisis, the Kaiser had certainly not discouraged the Austrian aggression. And now many of Germany's leaders, from the Kaiser on down, saw in the coming war an opportunity to improve Germany's power and influence. In response to the Russian partial mobilization on July 30, Germany began a general mobilization. With Germany mobilizing, Russian military authorities decided that their own general mobilization could be delayed no longer. That afternoon they convinced the reluctant Czar to issue the necessary orders. On July 31, Germany sent Russia an ultimatum to cease mobilizing within twelve hours. Russia refused and on the afternoon of August 1, 1914, Germany declared war on Russia.

Meanwhile, the German ambassador to France informed Prime Minister Viviani of Germany's ultimatum to Russia and asked whether or not France would remain neutral. Viviani responded that "France would act according to her interests." The German rightly interpreted this as meaning that France would honor her alliance with Russia, and so on August 3 Germany declared war on France. Immediately the modified Schlieffen Plan went into effect. German troops began to move into Belgium and Luxembourg.

That evening, in London, Sir Edward Grey sadly said: "The lamps are going out all over Europe; we shall not see them lit again in our lifetime." Since Britain was guarantor of Belgian neutrality, Grey next morning, August 4, sent an ultimatum to Germany demanding immediate withdrawal of troops from Belgian territory by midnight. German Chancellor von Bethmann-Hollweg pleaded in vain for Britain not to go to war for a mere "scrap of paper" — the treaty

19

Theobald von Bethmann-Hollweg, Chancellor of the German Empire. (Imperial War Museum)

Sir Edward Grey, Foreign Secretary of Great Britain. (U.S. Signal Corps)

assuring Belgian neutrality. But he would not order the invasion to halt. At midnight Great Britain declared war on Germany.

With one exception, the Triple Alliance and the Triple Entente were now locked in mortal combat. The exception was Italy, which declared that Austria's attack on Serbia did not apply to the defensive nature of the Triple Alliance. Italy, therefore, announced her neutrality.

Battles of the Frontiers

Liège

As modified by Moltke, the German war plan called for four great armies, totaling more than 1,200,000 men, to sweep through Belgium and Luxembourg in accordance with Schlieffen's concept. Since the neutrality of Holland was to be respected, this vast force had to advance on a front only 75 miles wide just as soon as the German mobilization was complete. The slightest delay would ruin the entire plan, because it would give the French time to realize their danger, and to shift their armies to meet the threat.

Directly in the path of the two German right-wing armies — the First and the Second — lay the great Belgian fortified area of Liège. The German plan could succeed only if Liège could be overwhelmed in the first two weeks of the war, while the First and Second Armies were completing their mobilization. The task was formidable, since Liège was one of the strongest and most modern fortified regions of Europe.

Mobilized German troops, in new field-gray uniforms, preparing to march into Belgium and France. (U.S. Signal Corps)

Thus the German plan called for an immediate attack against Liège by available troops of the Second Army at the very outbreak of war. On August 3 German troops began to cross the Belgian frontier, stimulating Britain's declaration of war. By August 5, six German brigades were assaulting the outer defenses of Liège, twelve powerful forts in a ring of twelve miles' diameter.

The Belgian army, some 165,000 strong, was mobilized by King Albert as soon as the Germans invaded. Albert assembled five of the army's six field divisions, about 80,000 men, midway between Brussels and Liège, hoping that the German advance would be sufficiently delayed by the fortresses of Liège and Namur to permit French and British troops to come to his assistance. His remaining

22

German 42-cm howitzer and crew. This type of gun — often called "Big Bertha," after Bertha von Krupp, wife of the great German munitions manufacturer — battered the forts of Liège into submission. (Imperial War Museum)

field division he placed under the command of General Gerard Leman, commanding Liège, to hold the intervals between the forts. This brought Leman's strength up to 40,000 men. Albert sent Leman an order to hold Liège "to the end." Leman obeyed.

During the afternoon of August 5, the Germans were repulsed in their efforts to penetrate between the Liège forts. But Leman now realized that one field division could not possibly hold the intervals against the overwhelming German force that was gathering against him. To keep the division from being annihilated, he decided that he would hold the forts with his 25,000 fortress troops as long as he possibly could; he sent the division back to join Albert's army on the Gette River.

Ruins of one of the Liège forts after the German bombardment. (U.S. Signal Corps)

General Gerard Leman (facing camera), heroic defender of Liège, returning in triumph from captivity after the war. (U.S. Signal Corps)

24

That night the Germans attacked again, and Leman again repulsed four of the five assaulting columns. One German brigade broke through, even though its commander had been killed in the attack. But General Erich Ludendorff, a senior general staff officer of the Second Army who was with the brigade, assumed command. During the next day and night, Ludendorff fought his way into Liège, and forced the citadel to surrender early on the seventh.

But the outer ring of twelve forts remained intact, and Leman scornfully rejected German demands that he surrender. Ludendorff and his brigade were now cut off. General Karl von Bülow, Second Army commander, brought up heavy siege artillery, while he threw more troops into the fight. On August 10, one of the outer forts was captured, and Ludendorff regained contact with the main army. The great German 17-inch siege howitzers, throwing shells weighing more than a ton, now systematically battered the remaining eleven forts into submission, one at a time.

Finally, on August 16, the last two battered forts were captured. Brave General Leman was found in the ruins, alive but unconscious. The Germans took him prisoner, but treated him as a hero. The German First and Second Armies at once began their march through the battered fortified region of Liège. Leman had delayed the German advance, but only for two or three days.

King Albert realized that he could do nothing to halt the advance of these two great German armies, totaling four times the strength of his own field forces. So, putting one mobile division into the fortifications of Namur, he retired into the fortified area of Antwerp, where he could keep communications with Britain open by sea. General Alexander von Kluck, commander of the German First Army, detached a corps to blockade Antwerp and to prevent the

Bridge over the Meuse River at Liège, destroyed by the Belgians during the siege. (U.S. Signal Corps)

Belgians from attacking his line of communications through Belgium. On August 20, Kluck's army entered Brussels, continuing its great sweep to the west toward Lille.

Battle of Lorraine

Meanwhile, as covering forces skirmished inside Alsace, the French armies completed their mobilization. On August 14, they began to carry out Plan XVII. The right-wing Army of Alsace, under General Paul Pau, advanced steadily to capture Mulhouse on the nineteenth. To his left, the main French offensive effort was launched into Lor-

26

raine, southeast of Metz, by the First and Second Armies. By August 18 the spearheads of General Auguste Dubail's First Army had reached Sarrebourg, while General Noël de Castelnau's Second Army was at Morhange. Here German resistance stiffened.

The Germans had been withdrawing slowly in front of the French, according to plan, and six reserve corps, which were eventually intended to bolster the right wing, were now temporarily assigned by Moltke to his left-wing armies. On August 20, General Josias von Heeringen's Seventh Army, and Prince Rupprecht of Bavaria's Sixth Army, turned suddenly in violent converging counterattacks, catching the advancing French completely by surprise. After a day of savage fighting the French were defeated all along the line. The First Army withdrew in good order, but the right wing of the Second Army was shattered. By August 22 it was driven back in confusion to the line of the Meurthe River at Lunéville. The army was saved by the magnificent defensive stand of General Ferdinand Foch's XX Corps on the fortified heights west of the frontier and east of the Meurthe River, above Nancy.

When Moltke learned of the great successes won by his left-wing armies, he decided that the French First and Second Armies had been smashed, and approved the requests of the Sixth and Seventh Army commanders to continue their offensives. He also agreed to leave the six extra reserve corps with the left wing, and to modify the Schlieffen Plan by making a double envelopment.

Battle of the Ardennes

Under Plan XVII, the three French left-wing armies were supposed to undertake an offensive which would pass north of Metz. Just be-

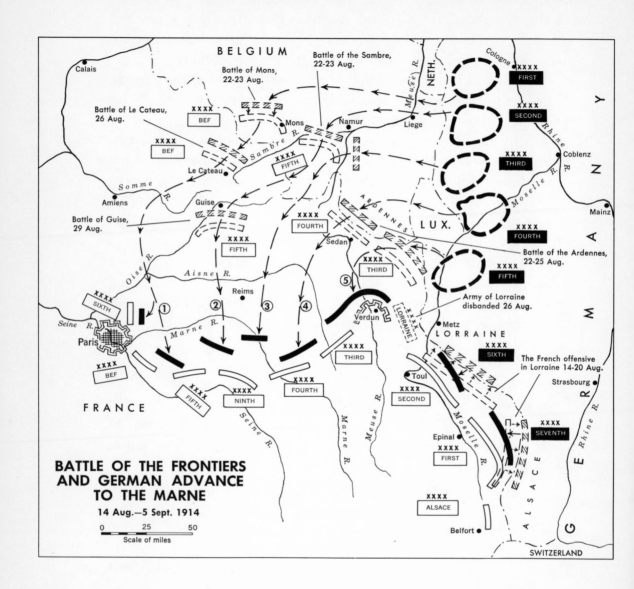

BELGIUM

Calais

Battle of Mons,
22-23 Aug.

Battle of the Sambre,
22-23 Aug.

Cologne

XXXX
FIRST

XXXX BEF

Mons

Namur

Liege

XXXX
SECOND

Coblenz

Rhine R.

Meuse R.

NETH.

Battle of Le Cateau,
26 Aug.

XXXX BEF

Sambre R.

XXXX
FIFTH

XXXX
THIRD

Le Cateau

Somme R.

Moselle R.

Amiens

Guise

ARDENNES

XXXX
FOURTH

Sedan

LUX.

Mainz

XXXX
FOURTH

Battle of Guise,
29 Aug.

XXXX
FIFTH

Aisne R.

Reims

XXXX
THIRD

Battle of the Ardennes,
22-25 Aug.

XXXX
FIFTH

Oise R.

①

②

③

④

⑤

Verdun

X X X
LORRAINE

Army of Lorraine
disbanded 26 Aug.

XXXX
SIXTH

Seine R.

Paris

Marne R.

Metz

LORRAINE

XXXX
SIXTH

The French offensive
in Lorraine 14-20 Aug.

XXXX BEF

XXXX
THIRD

Toul

Strasbourg

FRANCE

XXXX
FIFTH

XXXX
NINTH

Seine R.

XXXX
FOURTH

Meuse R.

Marne R.

XXXX
SECOND

Moselle R.

XXXX
SEVENTH

Epinal

Rhine R.

XXXX
FIRST

ALSACE

BATTLE OF THE FRONTIERS
AND GERMAN ADVANCE
TO THE MARNE
14 Aug.—5 Sept. 1914

0   25   50
Scale of miles

XXXX
ALSACE

Belfort

SWITZERLAND

28

fore they were scheduled to attack, General Charles Lanrezac, commanding the Fifth Army, persuaded Joffre that the Germans were moving into Belgium in tremendous strength. On August 15 Lanrezac was permitted to shift west of the Meuse River, and to advance into Belgium as far as the Sambre River. The Fourth Army, under General Fernand de Langle de Cary, which had been in reserve, was moved into the position vacated by the Fifth. On August 20 the Fourth and the Third (commanded by General Pierre X. E. Ruffey) began the planned offensive, but with the direction of their advance toward the northeast, into the Ardennes region of Luxembourg and eastern Belgium, instead of eastward as originally planned. They hoped to be able to get through the difficult, mountainous Ardennes Forest before meeting opposition.

On August 22 the French and German Fourth Armies met in headlong collision in the middle of the rugged forest region. At the same time, Crown Prince Wilhelm's Fifth Army, pivot of the Schlieffen Plan maneuver, struck the French Third Army in front and flank. There followed three days of confused and furious fighting, with the outnumbered French returning to attack after each repulse. By August 24 the French Third Army was shattered, and reeling back toward the fortress of Verdun. The Fourth Army, in only slightly better condition, was withdrawing across the Meuse, north and south of Sedan, closely followed by Duke Albrecht of Württemberg's German Fourth Army.

Joffre's Plan XVII had crumbled. The French doctrine of "offensive to the utmost" had been drowned in blood. The Germans thought that the French army and its morale had been smashed as thoroughly as its plan and its doctrine.

Battle of the Sambre

Lanrezac's Fifth Army arrived in the angle between the Sambre and the Meuse rivers on August 20, just as the German Second Army was probing the outer defenses of Namur, and General Max von Hausen's Third Army was approaching Dinant. General von Bülow, who had been given authority to coordinate the operations of the three right-wing armies, ordered a combined converging attack of the Second and Third Armies on Lanrezac's Fifth for August 22. Meanwhile, he pushed across the Sambre, taking advantage of French delay in organizing the defense of that river. During the afternoon of the twenty-first, battle became general just south of the Sambre as the French counterattacked, and halted the German advance.

On August 22, as furious fighting continued south of the Sambre, Lanrezac planned to envelop Bülow's left flank the next morning, and withdrew units from the Meuse River for this purpose. He requested British Field Marshal Sir John French, commanding the British Expeditionary Force on his left, to cooperate in what Lanrezac hoped would be a double envelopment. To Lanrezac's annoyance the British commander refused; nevertheless, he continued with his plan. The weakening of the French right, however, permitted Hausen's army to force its way across the Meuse River, late on the twenty-second, as Lanrezac was preparing for his counterattack on the twenty-third. Just as that attack was about to be delivered by General Franchet d'Esperey's I Corps, the German Third Army began to advance, threatening Lanrezac's right. In desperate fighting throughout the day, the French halted both of the converging German attacks, but Lanrezac knew that he could not hold another day. That night, with Joffre's permission, he withdrew in good order.

Arrival of the British Expeditionary Force in France. A troop train at Rouen, August 18, 1914, en route to Le Cateau. (Imperial War Museum)

Battle of Mons

The British Expeditionary Force, under Field Marshal French, had efficiently crossed the Channel in early August, and concentrated near Le Cateau, left of the French Fifth Army. Man for man, this British professional army was probably the best in the world at that time. But, because of its size, Kaiser Wilhelm had been at least partly right when he referred to it as "a contemptible little army." Yet these 125,000 men, already proudly calling themselves "the Contemptibles" (later, "the Old Contemptibles"), were to play a major role in the coming operations. Sir John French had been instructed to cooperate with his French allies, but to retain his army

Field Marshal Sir John French. (U.S. Signal Corps)

as an independent force. The future of allied cooperation was threatened, however, when Field Marshal French and General Lanrezac
met, in mid-August, and found they did not like each other.

Upon Joffre's request, the British, on August 21, moved into Belgium to conform to Lanrezac's advance to the Sambre. Next day
Sir John French, arriving at Mons, refused Lanrezac's request to join
in a double envelopment of the German Second Army. This was not
for pettiness, as Lanrezac assumed, but because British reconnaissance airplanes had informed Sir John that there was a large German
force approaching from the north.

General von Kluck's First Army, which had been heading generally westward, had on the twenty-first obeyed an order from Bülow to shift its direction of advance to the southward. This was partly because of Bülow's preparations for the Battle of the Sambre, and partly because both Kluck and Bülow had received a false report that the British had not yet arrived in France. So they assumed that there was no need to sweep farther to the west to complete their envelopment of the French armies, according to the Schlieffen Plan.

Early on the morning of August 23, the German First Army smashed head on into the British Expeditionary Force at Mons, and came to a grinding halt. The Germans were totally unprepared for the deadliness of the British infantry's aimed rifle fire. Their casualties were so heavy that they thought they were opposed by an army of machine gunners.

General von Kluck, however, was perhaps the most aggressive and dynamic of the German army commanders. After a brief pause he renewed his attack, with better coordination of infantry and artillery. By nightfall the outnumbered British had been driven back three miles. But Field Marshal French and his troops knew they had hurt the Germans far more severely than they themselves had suffered. British morale was high, and French was prepared to renew the battle on August 24. That night, however, he learned of the withdrawal of Lanrezac's Fifth Army, and realized that he would have to retire also, or else be isolated and overwhelmed. Because French thought that Lanrezac had deliberately abandoned him, without adequate notice of his intention to withdraw, the already strained relations between these two Allied generals became bitter.

The Results

By August 26 the French offensive had failed completely, at a cost of more than 300,000 casualties. But Moltke overestimated the extent of the German victory. His communications with his armies were poor, and his information was faulty. Believing that the success in Lorraine was a decisive victory, and thinking he could now complete a double envelopment, he ordered his left-wing armies to continue their offensive against the fortified Nancy heights. This was the very thing Schlieffen had wished to avoid at all costs.

Moltke also considered that the Ardennes–Sambre battles had been decisive, and so he ordered his right-wing armies to continue their sickle-like sweep. Confident that the French armies were on the verge of destruction, he even detached two corps from the right wing to hasten by railroad to the Eastern Front, to meet an unexpected Russian threat. Because of this, and because of other detachments to blockade the Belgians at Antwerp and the French garrison of Maubeuge, the three right-wing German armies had been bled from a strength of sixteen corps to eleven. And the reserve reinforcements planned for these armies had been retained in Lorraine. The Schlieffen Plan, already watered down from the original concept of its creator, was now almost unrecognizable. Nevertheless, the right-wing armies were still powerful, and were still advancing as Schlieffen had planned.

Joffre had kept more closely in touch with his subordinates than had Moltke, and he was well aware of the actual situation. He knew that, despite tactical defeat, the morale of his troops was still high. The German plan was also clearly revealed to him now.

German Advance to the Marne

The Plans

Seemingly oblivious of the disastrous failure of his Plan XVII, Joffre on August 25 calmly prepared for a counterattack. This would be a Schlieffen Plan in reverse, pivoting about the fortified area at Verdun. In Alsace and Lorraine, Joffre ordered his First and Second Armies to hold at all costs. While the Third, Fourth, and Fifth Armies, and the BEF, were to continue their southwesterly withdrawals, Joffre drew units from his embattled right wing, and from reserves in the interior of France, to create two new armies. The Sixth, under General Michel J. Maunoury, was to assemble near Amiens — which Joffre expected would be west of the German right wing — prepared to attack eastward. The Ninth, under General Foch, would fill a gap between the Fourth and Fifth Armies, and would provide weight for a general counterattack when the Allied left-wing armies had fallen back to the general line of the Somme River–Verdun.

Moltke, whose headquarters was still at Coblenz, more than 100 miles from the closest part of the front, ordered his five right-wing armies to continue their great wheel to get behind the French armies. The First Army was to turn westward again, to swing around Paris; the Second was to head generally toward Paris; the other armies were to sweep east of the city. The Sixth and Seventh Armies were to continue their attacks toward the Moselle, to complete the great double envelopment.

Battle of Le Cateau

During the Battles of the Frontiers, all the German armies, except the Third, had suffered heavy losses. These losses, combined with fatigue from long and fast marching, had caused some slackening of the pace of the German advance. On the extreme German right, however, the indomitable Kluck — whose First Army had marched farthest and hardest — drove relentlessly in pursuit of the BEF. The BEF was thus forced to fight almost continual rearguard actions. Kluck was trying to envelop the British left flank, to cut them off from the Channel ports. Therefore, the British left wing — the II Corps under General Horace Smith-Dorrien — was under greater pressure than was General Douglas Haig's I Corps on the right. Smith-Dorrien's corps had also suffered heavier losses at Mons.

On the night of August 25, the II Corps occupied a position west of Le Cateau. That night, Sir John French ordered the retreat to continue the next day, but Smith-Dorrien knew that he could not avoid a battle with the Germans unless he could get away before daylight. This would mean that some of his units, which had been fighting rearguard actions most of the day, would get no rest, and most would have only a few hours. He believed that this would be making a greater demand on his troops than they could endure. Furthermore, the roads behind his corps were clogged with fugitives, and with some French units moving to cover the Allied left flank. Therefore, he notified Sir John French that he intended to stop on the twenty-sixth, holding off the Germans during the day, and then withdraw after dark the following night.

French understood the reason for Smith-Dorrien's decision, yet he also recognized the danger of any delay in withdrawal. So he

General Sir Horace L. Smith-Dorrien, commander of the British II Corps in the Marne Campaign, in a photograph taken after the war. (Imperial War Museum)

ordered Haig's corps to retire as planned, and urged Smith-Dorrien to continue the retreat, but told him to do what he thought best.

Kluck, not expecting the BEF to halt on the twenty-sixth, unexpectedly ran into the II Corps early in the morning. He immediately attacked. The British I Corps had begun marching southward before dawn, as ordered. This left Smith-Dorrien's right flank completely exposed. The British center held firm against the German attacks, but Kluck's wings began to lap around the II Corps' flanks. Smith-Dorrien threw in all of his reserves to hold the flanks, but to no avail. To avoid encirclement, Smith-Dorrien had to disengage during daylight. He was able to accomplish this with the help of a series of gallant attacks by a nearby French cavalry corps. In the process, Smith-Dorrien lost most of his artillery. British casualties

British cavalry during the retreat from Mons. (Imperial War Museum)

were about 8,000 men out of 40,000 in action. German losses were somewhat greater. Kluck's casualties prevented him from pursuing vigorously and the British broke contact during the night.

While Le Cateau was a successful delaying action, it was a totally unnecessary one. Smith-Dorrien's troops not only got no rest, they had to fight and suffer heavy losses as well. Responsibility for the defeat belongs to French who should have either ordered Smith-Dorrien to retreat, or else made Haig's corps stand and fight also.

Battle of Guise

When Joffre received exaggerated reports of the British defeat at Le Cateau, he feared that his counterattack plans were threatened.

Unless the BEF could remain intact to delay the German right wing, and later to take part in the counteroffensive, he might not have time or units to build up the striking force now assembling near Amiens. On August 27, to relieve pressure on the British, he ordered Lanrezac's Fifth Army to attack to the northwest, striking at Kluck's left flank.

Lanrezac knew that he was being closely followed by Bülow's Second Army. Reluctantly, however, he planned to shift the front of most of his army by 90 degrees, from northeast to northwest. Lanrezac's plan was to attack west across the Oise River, toward St.-Quentin, with two corps, while defending the original army front with one corps. He kept one corps in reserve to support in either direction. He asked the British to make a limited attack northward to hold the German First Army in place during his planned attack.

Colonel General Alexander von Kluck, commander of the German First Army in the Marne Campaign. (U.S. Signal Corps)

Colonel General Karl von Bülow, commander of the German Second Army in the Marne Campaign. (U.S. Signal Corps)

Field Marshal French refused. Since Lanrezac's attack was for the purpose of taking pressure off the BEF, French believed he should be able to take full advantage of this opportunity to rest his troops. This foolish and short-sighted refusal increased the distrust already existing between French and Lanrezac. French could easily have helped by committing some units from Haig's I Corps.

On the morning of August 29, Bülow's Second Army ran into the French delaying positions along the upper Oise before Lanrezac's attack to the west could get started. By the early afternoon the German Second Army was driving French troops back in the north, while the two corps which had been supposed to attack westward were instead defending the line of the Oise River. There was no impact at all on Kluck's First Army, which had been the entire purpose of the operation. Lanrezac now committed his reserve, the I Corps, under General Louis Franchet d'Esperey, to counterattack northward in the center of the original line. Carefully prepared, Franchet d'Esperey's attack struck violently shortly before sundown. The center of Bülow's army was hurled back in great disorder, although the Germans were able to maintain themselves south of the Oise until darkness ended the battle.

Lanrezac had done a good job of preparing his army for battle, but had exercised little control once the fighting began. Had he employed Franchet d'Esperey to envelop Bülow's exposed left flank, he might have ruined the whole German plan. As it was, Bülow's army was badly hurt, but Lanrezac had to retreat to avoid being flanked by the unhindered German First Army. The battle had accomplished Joffre's purpose, however, since pressure had been reduced on the BEF. Furthermore, Bülow's army was so badly hurt that he was unable to advance on the thirtieth. Lanrezac broke contact to withdraw safely.

Kluck's First Dilemma

By August 30, Kluck had driven his First Army well south of the Somme River to the vicinity of Roye. That same day he received a message from Bülow asking him to move southeast instead of southwest to help exploit the "decisive victory" the Second Army had gained at Guise.

The request from Bülow put Kluck in a dilemma. He was no longer under Bülow's command, and his orders from Moltke two days earlier had directed him to advance to the Seine west of Paris. But the orders had also assigned him several other missions: to be prepared to go to the aid of Bülow's Second Army; to protect the German right flank; and to prevent the formation of enemy units to the west.

41

Kluck was convinced that he had eliminated the British from the campaign; he had also scattered the small French units which had appeared on the German right flank. Thus two of his subsidiary missions seemed to have been fully accomplished, and his cavalry could continue to cover the flank adequately. He was unable to make radio contact with Moltke, whose GHQ had now moved to Luxembourg. Fearing that he might lose an opportunity to smash the French Fifth Army — which he assumed was the only major unit remaining on the Allied left flank — Kluck decided to move to the southeast in response to Bülow's request. Although this change of direction would bring his army east of Paris, he considered he was carrying out Moltke's intentions. He was confirmed in this opinion when he later learned that Bülow's army was not moving on August 31, despite the claims of a great victory.

By this time, Joffre realized that he would be unable to halt and counterattack along the Somme–Verdun line as he had planned. So he ordered the retreat to continue, now intending to establish a line between Paris and Verdun, from which he could strike the counterblow. His airplanes and his cavalry reported the change of direction of the German First Army early on the thirty-first. This confirmed his ideas for a new plan.

On September 1, Joffre issued new and detailed instructions. The withdrawing armies were to continue their retreat, if necessary to the line of the Seine River, to form an arc between Paris and Verdun. At the same time Maunoury's Sixth Army would assemble in and around Paris. If Kluck continued to the southeast, the Sixth Army would attack eastward against the German right flank; if Kluck shifted back to the west, Maunoury would attack westward against the First Army's left flank, cutting him off from the remaining German armies.

The British Attitude

Joffre's principal concern at this time was whether or not he could count on the wholehearted participation of Sir John French and the BEF in the planned counteroffensive. Whichever side of Paris Kluck's army came, Joffre planned to have the German advance blocked by the British, while Maunoury's Sixth Army struck Kluck's flank from Paris. But Sir John, wrongly convinced that his troops had suffered more than most French units, had decided that he could not fight another major battle until his army had rested and received reinforcements to make up for its losses at Mons and Le Cateau. Furthermore, his distrust and dislike for Lanrezac now colored his attitude toward all French generals. Apparently ignoring Joffre's requests to fit into the planned counterattack, he was withdrawing southward, just east of Paris, as rapidly as his tired troops could march.

Rumors of this state of affairs had reached the British Cabinet, and Lord Horatio H. Kitchener, the British Secretary of State for War, sent a telegram to French, asking if the BEF was conforming to Joffre's plan. In response Sir John cabled: "I have no definite idea of General Joffre's general plan; its general result is the advance of the Germans and the retreat of the Allies."

Kitchener hastened to Paris, where he conferred with Joffre. Then, on September 1, he sent for Sir John French. What went on between these two old British soldiers has never been reported. In any event, the very next day French sent a message to Joffre, suggesting that the time had come for the Allies to stand and fight. Joffre now knew that he could rely upon wholehearted British cooperation with his plan.

Field Marshal Lord Horatio H. Kitchener, British Secretary of State for War. (Imperial War Museum)

General Michel J. Maunoury, commander of the French Sixth Army during the Battle of the Marne. (U.S. Signal Corps)

44

Kluck's Second Dilemma

On August 31 and the first two days of September, Kluck drove southeast as fast as he could push his army. Since Bülow's halt after Guise had put the Second Army a full day's march behind him, Kluck believed that he could hit the French Fifth Army from the flank while Bülow engaged it from the front. The French left wing would be rolled up, assuring the success of the Schlieffen Plan. By evening of September 2, units of Kluck's left-flank corps had reached the Marne River at Château-Thierry, at least 10 miles behind the left flank of the French Fifth Army, which in turn was at least 15 miles south of Bülow's right flank. Kluck's right flank and center corps were between the Oise and Ourcq rivers, hotly pursuing the British, who had reached the Marne just east of Paris.

Kluck was therefore amazed that same evening when he received orders from Moltke that his army was supposed to *follow* the Second Army in echelon, and to protect the German right flank while marching east of Paris. Moltke, having learned about the French buildup near Paris, still intended to carry out the Schlieffen Plan on a reduced scale. Kluck was to block the French forces in Paris while the other German armies continued the envelopment. Moltke did not realize, however, that Kluck was already far ahead of Bülow. What was worse, he failed to notify Kluck of the French buildup in Paris.

Kluck was now faced with a second dilemma. In order to follow the orders from GHQ he would have to halt his army for at least two days to let Bülow catch up. He had no indication of any great French strength in Paris. He also believed that because of Bülow's delay after Le Cateau, his own First Army was the only one which could accomplish Moltke's stated purpose of driving the French away from Paris. The next morning, while trying to decide what to do

45

about these orders, he was notified that his IX Corps had crossed the Marne River at Château-Thierry and was continuing to advance southward against light resistance. Still unable to communicate with Moltke, Kluck decided to push across the Marne with at least three corps, to carry out what seemed to be Moltke's intentions. He would leave two corps north of the Marne to block any possible threat from Paris.

Allied Preparation for Battle

By September 3, Kluck's characteristically bold move had confirmed Joffre's estimate of German intentions. He now realized that his Sixth Army could attack eastward from Paris against Kluck's right flank. Since his right-wing armies had decisively repulsed the vain assaults of the German Sixth and Seventh Armies, he decided that his right could continue to hold at reduced strength. He therefore withdrew more units from the right to reinforce his Sixth and Ninth Armies.

To be certain that his plans would be carried out faithfully and vigorously, Joffre now relieved a number of senior commanders who had good peacetime records, but who had not performed well in the fighting thus far. The most notable instance was the replacement of Lanrezac by the aggressive Franchet d'Esperey, hero of Guise. Franchet d'Esperey got along well with Field Marshal French, thus assuring vital coordination between the BEF and the Fifth Army.

Joffre also saw to it that his retreating units, now approaching their home depots, were brought up to full strength with replacements. Thus, while the tired German units, at the end of their long lines of communications, were daily dwindling in strength, the de-

46

pleted French units now received enough replacements to make up for most of their combat losses to date. The Allies thus had a clear numerical superiority between Verdun and Paris.

On September 2 the French government moved from Paris to Bordeaux. Winston Churchill, then a member of the British Government, reported that he and his Cabinet colleagues were cheered by this, since it "showed a resolve to treat the capital just as if it were an ordinary tactical feature. . . . It also showed a resolve to continue the war, no matter what might happen to Paris."

This impression was confirmed by the attitude and actions of elderly General Joseph S. Gallieni, military governor of Paris. He used all available soldier and civilian labor to restore to full fighting condition the strong but neglected fortifications surrounding the city. He issued a proclamation that Paris would be held "to the bitter end," and prepared to demolish the city if it should ever become necessary to surrender or to retreat. During the assembly of Maunoury's Sixth Army in the fortified region of Paris, it was under Gallieni's command.

Moltke's New Plan

By this time Moltke had received reports from his armies on the eastern and central part of the front that their reconnaissance airplanes could see great shifts of French troops to the west by road and railroad. And his spies were sending him quite accurate reports of events in Paris. He was therefore convinced that his right-wing armies, fatigued after their long marches and hard battles, and without replacements, could no longer overpower the Allied forces in and around Paris. His central armies, however, had seen little serious

A statue of General Joseph S. Gallieni, Military Governor of Paris during the Battle of the Marne; the statue was erected in his honor after the war by the city of Paris. (U.S. Signal Corps)

action since the Battle of the Ardennes, and the Third had hardly fought at all.

On September 4, therefore, Moltke issued new orders, completely discarding the Schlieffen Plan. The First and Second Armies were to halt their advance and protect the German right flank, while the Third, Fourth, and Fifth Armies smashed through the extended French center, and the Sixth and Seventh Armies renewed their offensive against the weakened French defenses in Lorraine and Vosges. Moltke did not think it necessary to inform his subordinate commanders of the reasons for his changed orders.

Kluck was again astounded when he received orders that his army was to face Paris from positions between the Oise and Marne rivers.

By this time, four of his five corps were south of the Marne, and approaching the Seine, with only his IV Reserve Corps north of the Marne, near Meaux. Having no inkling of what was going on in Paris, or of the reasons for the new orders, Kluck again assumed that Moltke had no idea of what was happening at the front, and stubbornly he continued his advance.

Late on September 5, however, a staff officer from GHQ reached Kluck's headquarters, south of the Marne. He explained the situation to Kluck, who immediately realized the threat to his army and to the entire German group of armies. He ordered two corps to move back across the Marne the next day. He decided to wait for further developments before shifting all of his army back, since the staff officer assured him that there was no need for haste.

The Battle of the Marne

Joffre's Plan and Instructions

On September 4, General Joffre issued his final instructions for the counteroffensive. The Sixth Army was to advance eastward from Paris, north of the Marne, to cross the Ourcq River early on September 6. That same morning, the BEF, which had halted east of Paris, between the Seine and Marne rivers, was to advance northeastward, toward Montmirail; the Fifth Army, north of the Seine near Provins, was to make a converging attack northwestward toward Montmirail. Joffre expected that the attacks of these three armies would catch the German First Army in a double envelopment.

General Joffre, during an inspection of the front. (Imperial War Museum)

The Ninth, Fourth, and Third French Armies, which extended generally northeastward toward Verdun, were also to attack in a general northerly-northwesterly direction on September 6. The First and Second Armies were to hold their defensive positions around Nancy and in the Vosges.

Joffre, and every man in the Allied armies, knew well that the war would be lost if this attack failed. For the first time Joffre issued a general order to be read to all troops, telling them that "the time for looking backward had passed," and that the safety of France depended upon their efforts.

Battle of the Ourcq

In order to jump off across the Ourcq on September 6, Maunoury had started moving eastward from Paris early on the fifth. General Hans von Gronau, commanding the German IV Reserve Corps, had been left in the region between the Oise and the Marne by Kluck. He was marching slowly southward toward Meaux, when he received reports of activity on his right flank. Having no aviation and little cavalry for reconnaissance, Gronau decided to attack westward to find out what was going on.

Gronau's bold attack ran head on into Maunoury's army, which was not expecting to fight until the next day. By nightfall the French had been driven back several miles west of Meaux. Gronau realized, however, that he was up against a superior, though disorganized, force. Accordingly, he prudently withdrew to a strong, defensive position, and sent an urgent message to Kluck.

Gronau's attack had revealed Joffre's plan prematurely and probably saved the German First Army from a disastrous surprise blow on the sixth. But Kluck, not realizing the extent of the French strength, sent only one corps north to help Gronau.

Despite the surprise setback of the previous day, Maunoury attacked on the sixth, attempting to envelop Gronau's north flank, but the arrival of additional German units extended the line of battle, now running almost north and south, and overlapped the French north flank. Maunoury brought up more troops and continued attacking on the seventh, again attempting to envelop the German north flank. That same morning Kluck received a message from Moltke that removed all doubt as to French intentions north of the Marne. A copy of Joffre's attack order, picked up on the battlefield,

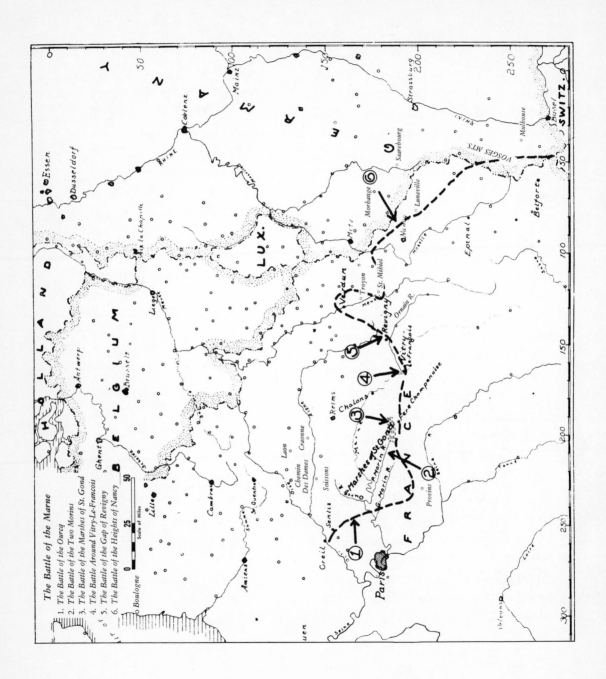

The Battle of the Marne

1. The Battle of the Ourcq
2. The Battle of the Two Morins
3. The Battle of the Marshes of St. Gond
4. The Battle Around Vitry-Le-Francois
5. The Battle of the Gap of Revigny
6. The Battle of the Heights of Nancy

made it clear that Maunoury was conducting a major offensive. As Kluck had the mission of protecting the right flank of the German armies, it was his responsibility to deal with this offensive. He decided, with characteristic boldness, to assemble the entire First Army north of the Marne and to remove the threat of Maunoury's army by completely defeating it. He thought the British had retreated too far to interfere with this operation.

Meanwhile, Maunoury pressed his attacks vigorously on the seventh and eighth. Gallieni rushed reinforcements to him from Paris, including two regiments of infantry sent in taxicabs. (Contrary to popular impression, this first spectacular movement of troops to a battlefield by motor did not have an important influence on the battle.) These reinforcements were offset by the arrival of other

Paris buses and taxicabs carrying French soldiers to the front. (United Press International)

German corps from the south, and on the evening of September 8, despite French numerical superiority, Kluck ordered a coordinated attack for the following day. Maunoury, having no more reserves, at the same time decided to pass to the defensive.

Battle of the Two Morins

Other events were taking place farther south and east while Maunoury and Kluck were fighting this fierce battle on the Ourcq. On September 6, the French Fifth Army had advanced to the north in accordance with the plan. The French troops met only rearguard delays from two of Kluck's corps, which were retreating across the Marne to help Gronau. This withdrawal exposed the right wing of Bülow's Second Army, which on the seventh received the full force of the French Fifth Army. Bülow pulled back his right flank behind the Petit-Morin River to avoid envelopment. This left a gap of 25 miles between the German First and Second Armies — a gap filled only by two small German cavalry corps.

The British army, getting off to a slow start, began moving into this gap on the seventh. The Fifth Army had also been slow in following the withdrawal of Bülow's right flank, but Franchet d'Esperey vigorously attacked the line of the Petit-Morin during the afternoon of the eighth, without success. That night, however, he tried a surprise night attack which was so successful that before dawn Bülow was forced to withdraw his right flank about 6 more miles to a position facing almost west.

Bülow's change of position still further widened the gap between the German First and Second Armies. By dawn of September 9,

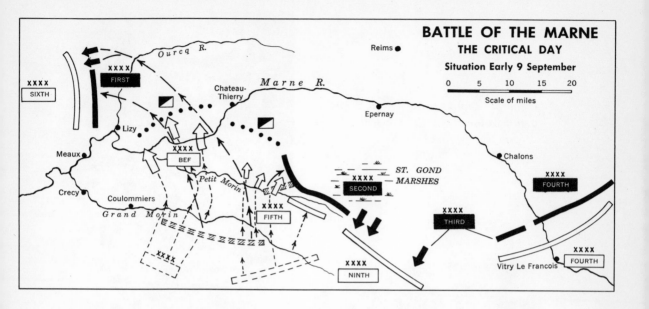

French's BEF was crossing the Marne River, pushing aside the skill-ful but woefully inadequate opposition of the German cavalry. After taking three days to traverse 25 miles, the British were at last nearing Kluck's rear, and Franchet d'Esperey was in a position to envelop Bülow's right flank. These movements could not succeed, however, unless Foch's Ninth Army could hold the center of the Allied line against the German main effort.

Battle of the St.-Gond Marshes

According to Moltke's new plan, the German Second Army was supposed to face Paris between the Marne and the Seine, which meant that Bülow had to swing his army at right angles, so that it

General Louis Franchet d'Esperey, commander of the French Fifth Army during the Battle of the Marne, in pre-war full-dress uniform. (U.S. Signal Corps)

General Ferdinand Foch, commander of the French Ninth Army during the Battle of the Marne, in prewar full-dress uniform. (U.S. Signal Corps)

56

faced west instead of south. While Bülow was starting to do this on the sixth, his left wing was suddenly struck by the left wing of Foch's Ninth Army, attacking north. Meanwhile, Hausen's German Third Army, driving south according to plan, ran into Foch's right wing, southwest of Châlons, early on the seventh.

The left wing and center of the Ninth Army had started their advance from the St.-Gond Marshes. But Foch's right wing extended southeastward from the marshes about 12 miles into flat, open plains. The left flank was protected by the advancing Fifth Army, but to the right there was a gap of 12 miles between Foch's Ninth and Langle de Cary's Fourth Army. Fortunately for both Foch and Langle, Hausen had detached nearly half of his army — his entire left wing — to assist Duke Albrecht of Württemberg's Fourth German Army. As a result there was a 12-mile gap in the middle of the German Third Army, exactly matching the gap in the French line.

The initial shock of the clash between Bülow's left wing and the left wing and center of Foch's army forced the French to fall back to better defensive positions in and behind the marshes. There they held, during bitter conflict, all through September 7. At the same time, Hausen's advance seriously endangered Foch's right wing, but here, too, the French held on, thanks to the extremely effective fire of their light artillery against the massed German formations in the open fields.

Frustrated by the skill and accuracy of the French artillery, Hausen launched a surprise night attack of four divisions at 3:00 A.M. the next day. The right wing of the Ninth Army reeled back in confusion. At this point Foch ordered his right-wing divisions to attack. Despite their amazement at this order, the French commanders did what they were told. The Germans, already thinking

57

French light field artillery in action; the 75-mm gun on the left has just been fired and is in full recoil. (United Press International)

Troops of the British Expeditionary Force crossing the Marne River on September 10, 1914, in their advance between the German First and Second Armies. (Imperial War Museum)

they had won, were equally amazed. The French attacks were weak, they were poorly organized, and they gained practically no ground. But they accomplished Foch's objective. By afternoon of the eighth, the German advance was halted, and the French retreat was stopped.

There is a legend in the French army that it was about this time that Foch reported his situation to Joffre. There is no copy in the records, but every Frenchman believes that Foch telegraphed: "My center is falling back. My right retreats. Situation excellent! I attack!"

French determination, exploited to its maximum by a general who understood his men, saved the day. The Germans, exhausted from their long marches and the vicious fighting, were unable to gain any more ground.

Vitry-le-François

The French Fourth Army, under General Langle de Cary, had fallen back from the Battle of the Ardennes to the Ornain River — a small tributary of the Marne. They held a line from Vitry-le-François on the left, almost to Revigny on the right. In response to Joffre's order, Langle attacked on September 6, and immediately ran into a German attack, the result of Moltke's new plan. This was the Fourth Army, under Duke Albrecht of Württemberg, reinforced by nearly half of Hausen's Third Army.

Although the Germans had a slight numerical superiority, the French fought them to a standstill in three days of violent fighting. Langle was separated by large gaps from Foch's Ninth Army, on his left, and from General Maurice Sarrail's Third Army, on his right. Albrecht was aware of the situation, but got into an argument with the German Crown Prince, who commanded the Fifth Army, as to where and how such flank attacks should be made. During this debate, Albrecht's men smashed at the French in vain frontal attacks for three days. The argument was settled by evening of the ninth, but by that time events elsewhere on the front prevented the German envelopments planned for the tenth.

Revigny and Verdun

Early in September, when Joffre was making changes among the French leadership, he relieved General Ruffey, who had commanded the French Third Army in the Battle of the Ardennes, and replaced him with General Sarrail. During early September, the Third Army had fallen back, just southwest of Verdun, with its left flank at Revigny, and its right linked with the Verdun garrison.

In compliance with Joffre's order, Sarrail attacked on September 6, but, as elsewhere along the front, immediately ran head on into a full-scale German attack by the German Crown Prince's Fifth Army. Neither side could gain in the ensuing desperate struggle. The Crown Prince tried to envelop the French left at Revigny, but was unsuccessful, in part due to his disagreement with Duke Albrecht.

The Crown Prince then ordered a corps from his left wing — which was facing the Verdun fortress — to move around Verdun and to cross the Meuse River 20 miles farther south in order to strike Sarrail's army in the rear. The maneuver nearly succeeded, because the line of the Meuse was only lightly held by the French. But a French cavalry division, and the small garrison at Fort Troyon on the Meuse, held off repeated German attacks until reinforcements arrived, several days after the rest of the Battle of the Marne had ended.

Nancy and the Vosges

The depleted First and Second Armies were the only French forces not attacking on September 6. But they were as heavily engaged as any of Joffre's armies, holding off intensive assaults of the German Sixth and Seventh Armies, which had begun on the fourth. The principal German effort was made against Castelnau's Second Army, in an attempt to break through the defenses at Nancy itself.

Several times Castelnau feared that he would be unable to withstand the pressure, and asked Joffre's permission to withdraw. But the indomitable French commander in chief was more confident of his troops and of the strength of their positions, and ordered Castelnau to hold on. By September 10, Moltke realized that Schlieffen had been right about the difficulties of attacking in Lorraine, and ordered the offensive to stop.

The Hentsch Mission

Meanwhile, the decisive action of the campaign was taking place just east of Paris. During the first three days of the battle, Moltke issued no orders. Because of his distance from the fighting front, and because of poor communications, he did not have a clear picture of the situation. But, by September 8, reports and scattered messages made him aware of the gap between his First and Second Armies, and caused him to realize that the British were advancing into the gap.

Worried about this, and by other rumors and pessimistic, fragmentary reports, Moltke decided to send a trusted general-staff officer — Lieutenant Colonel Richard Hentsch — to inspect the front.

Why Moltke waited so long, under the existing circumstances, and why he used only one staff officer to act as his eyes and ears, is not known. Hentsch's orders were never written down, and it has never been clear exactly what mission was given to him orally by Moltke.

On September 8, Hentsch visited the headquarters of the Fifth, Fourth, and Third Armies. He sent back encouraging reports to Moltke. He arrived at Second Army headquarters after dark that evening, to find Bülow extremely depressed about the situation, and particularly about the threat to his right flank. Despite the successes which his army and Hausen's had achieved against Foch, he feared disaster to his army and that of Kluck unless both armies withdrew right away. While Bülow and Hentsch were discussing the situation, word was received of Franchet d'Esperey's successful night attack, still further endangering Bülow's right wing. Bülow thereupon ordered that wing to withdraw, although his left was to continue its attacks against Foch.

It is not clear whether or not Hentsch tried to persuade Bülow to change his mind about withdrawing the right wing. In any event, before the evening was over he had virtually approved the withdrawal in Moltke's name. Early the next morning, Hentsch rushed northwestward to Kluck's headquarters on the Ourcq River to inform him of the withdrawal of the Second Army, and of the Allied advance into the widening gap between the two armies. Kluck's early morning attack against Maunoury had already begun to make some progress, and Kluck was at the front, personally encouraging his troops. His chief of staff tried to get Hentsch's approval to continue the attack, but Hentsch — quite rightly — ordered an immediate withdrawal in Moltke's name. Had the First Army delayed just a few hours longer it would probably have been completely encircled.

The Results

Moltke ordered a general retirement, and the Germans quickly and efficiently retreated to a line running generally eastward from Noyon to Verdun, where they began to entrench themselves. The Allies followed slowly. They were too exhausted and too badly hurt by three weeks of incredibly intensive fighting and marching to undertake an aggressive pursuit.

So ended the Battle of the Marne, strategically the most decisive since Waterloo, ninety-nine years before. It was not a great tactical victory for the Allies, who lost about 250,000 men. German losses were somewhat higher, but their morale was not shattered. The German defeat was caused as much by their own moves — which created the gap and made their position untenable — as by the action of the Allies. Had they not retreated when they did, however, the Germans might have been completely defeated.

Yet the Germans came so close to overwhelming victory that it is interesting to consider what would have happened if they had acted somewhat differently. If Moltke had followed the Schlieffen Plan more closely at the outset, or had maintained better communication with and control over his armies, or if Hentsch had seen Kluck before he visited Bülow, the results might have been entirely different. The greatest speculation surrounds what would have happened had the two corps Moltke sent to East Prussia — or a similar number of troops committed to the vain attacks in Lorraine — been present on the Marne in early September. They could perhaps have filled the gap between Kluck and Bülow and opposed the advance of the BEF while Maunoury was being enveloped and Foch overwhelmed.

On the other hand, no matter what the Germans might have done, they would have had a difficult time. The solid determination of Joffre and the toughness and resiliency of the French soldier certainly played a part as important to the result as the exhaustion and confused leadership of the Germans. Almost equally important was the role played by the sound, professional British soldiery, far out of proportion to their relatively small numbers. Had they been employed more aggressively on September 6 and 7, they might have sealed the doom of Kluck's army.

From the mass of might-have-beens, one fact emerged above all. The victory had been planned and won by a strong, capable, resourceful leader, who never lost control of his subordinates. Joffre's reconstruction of a counterattack upon the wreckage of his initial plan was as masterful as it was amazing. Critics, finding it difficult to see a spark of genius in the corpulent, pedestrian figure, have attributed Joffre's calmness to a lack of imagination, and to a failure to realize the enormity of the catastrophe he had created. These critics attribute the French recovery to the intervention of the aristocratic, dramatic Gallieni, who is supposed to have stimulated Joffre to order the counteroffensive, and who supplied him the Sixth Army and the "taxicab reinforcements" which made it possible.

This is nonsense. Maunoury's army had been created by Joffre solely for the mission for which it was used, and the concept of the counteroffensive was fully developed in his mind long before events forced him to fall back to Paris to initiate it. Joffre may not have been one of the world's greatest military geniuses. But no general has ever handled vast armies better than he did between August 25 and September 9, 1914.

British machine gunner in the trenches during the First Battle of the Aisne. (Imperial War Museum)

The Race to the Sea*

First Battle of the Aisne

Moltke's last major decision as Chief of the German Army General Staff was a good one. Having lost the Battle of the Marne, he ordered his four right-flank armies to retreat to the easily defensible ridgeline north of the Aisne and Vesle rivers. At the same time, he halted the vain attacks of his Seventh Army against the French right

---

*As will be seen in this chapter, the operations which historians have called the "Race to the Sea" might more properly be designated "Leapfrog to the Flanks." The name has stuck, however, and we use it here.

65

General Erich von Falkenhayn, German Minister of War, and Chief of the German General Staff after the Battle of the Marne. (U.S. Signal Corps)

flank, and rushed it northwestward by railroad to the Chemin des Dames Ridge, behind the Aisne River. There it filled the gap still yawning between the First and Second Armies. These moves were completed on September 14, and the Germans began to entrench in preparation for the expected Allies' pursuit and counterattack. That same day Moltke was relieved of his duties as Chief of the General Staff by the Kaiser. He was replaced by General Erich von Falkenhayn, the German Minister of War.

The change was kept secret, in order to keep the German people from realizing how badly their army had failed at the Marne. Although Falkenhayn immediately assumed command, Moltke remained at the High Command headquarters for another month and a half. Until a suitable replacement was obtained for his cabinet post, early in 1915, Falkenhayn continued to serve as Minister of War, as well as Chief of the General Staff. At the same time, he exercised direct command over operations on the Western Front.

Although the Allies had not pursued the retreating Germans very vigorously, their cavalry and infantry patrols had followed closely behind the withdrawal. Allied spearheads began to cross the Aisne River on September 13. Joffre ordered a general offensive along the entire front against the new German line, to begin on September 14. The British, who had been less heavily engaged than most of the French armies during the Battle of the Marne, were to make the main effort, attacking the Chemin des Dames Ridge between Soissons and Craonne; their objective was Laon.

If the Allies had expected the Germans to be demoralized after their defeat on the Marne, these expectations were soon cruelly smashed. The Germans, better trained than the Allies for defensive operations, and more liberally equipped with machine guns, repulsed every assault, and repeatedly drove the Allies back in fierce counterattacks. On September 18 Joffre ordered a halt to the costly and useless offensive. It was obvious that his troops were unable to break through the carefully selected German trench line, anchored by machine guns, and supported by plentiful German medium and heavy artillery. The Allies had few big guns of their own to match these German weapons, which were able to stay far enough behind the front to be beyond the range of the French light artillery.

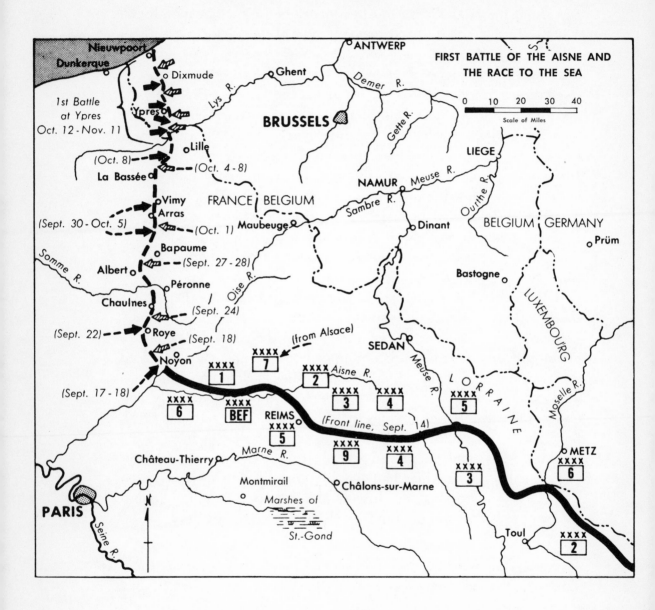

FIRST BATTLE OF THE AISNE AND
THE RACE TO THE SEA

0   10   20   30   40
Scale of Miles

Nieuwpoort
Dunkerque
o Dixmude
Ghent o
ANTWERP o

1st Battle
at Ypres
Oct. 12 - Nov. 11

Ypres

Lys R.

BRUSSELS

Demer R.

Gette R.

LIEGE

Lille
(Oct. 8)
(Oct. 4 - 8)
La Bassée

FRANCE BELGIUM

NAMUR

Meuse R.

Vimy
Arras
(Sept. 30 - Oct. 5)
(Oct. 1)
Maubeuge o

Sambre R.

Dinant o

BELGIUM GERMANY

Prüm o

Somme R.

Bapaume
(Sept. 27 - 28)
Albert o
Péronne o
Chaulnes
(Sept. 24)
(Sept. 22)
Roye o
(Sept. 18)
Noyon
(Sept. 17 - 18)

Oise R.

Bastogne o

LUXEMBOURG

(from Alsace)
SEDAN o

XXXX
7

XXXX
1

XXXX
2   Aisne R.

Meuse R.

XXXX
6

XXXX
BEF
REIMS

XXXX
3

XXXX
4

LORRAINE

XXXX
5

Moselle R.

Château-Thierry

Marne R.

XXXX
5

(Front line, Sept. 14)

XXXX
9

XXXX
4

METZ o

XXXX
6

PARIS

Seine R.

Montmirail o

Marshes of

Châlons-sur-Marne o

XXXX
3

St.-Gond

Toul o

XXXX
2

Battles of Picardy and Artois

Joffre now decided to envelop the exposed German right flank, then resting on the narrow Oise River. Local reserves of the French Sixth Army, and supporting cavalry units, began an attempt to get around the German flank near Noyon. At the same time, Joffre shifted Castelnau's Second Army from the Nancy front to extend the Allied left flank, so that it could become an encircling force.

But Falkenhayn had initiated a similar series of moves at the same time. The result was the bitterly contested Battle of Picardy, which lasted from September 22 through September 26. This resulted in an extension of the battle line to the northward, beyond the Somme, in the vicinity of Péronne and Albert. Losses were heavy on both sides; neither had been able to get around the other's flank; both the Allied and German northwestern flanks were still "in the air."

The Battle of Picardy was followed by more of the same kind of desperate, successive outflanking attempts by both the Allies and the Germans. On both sides the immediate objective of each effort was to try to turn the opponent's exposed flank. In the process, the line gradually, but inexorably, stretched farther north toward the North Sea. The flanks themselves were held mostly by cavalry units.

With the Allies' attention focused on the flanks, Falkenhayn permitted the Crown Prince to make another attempt to surround and capture Verdun. The German Fifth Army's attacks on September 22 were repulsed west of Verdun, but to the east they succeeded in taking St.-Mihiel on the twenty-fourth, pushing a deep salient into the Allied lines. From this salient they were able to place artillery fire on the roads to Verdun, and on the Paris–Nancy railroad. For four years the Germans would make the most of this favorable situation at St.-Mihiel. But Falkenhayn again shifted his attention back to the north.

On September 27 the arrival north of the Somme of reinforcements from Germany permitted Falkenhayn to undertake a new effort to get around the Allied left flank. Joffre rushed troops from the right of his line and from the interior of France to meet the new threat. The ensuing Battle of Artois raged until October 10. By this time the battle line had stretched northward to the Lys River at the frontier of Belgian and French Flanders.

During this process of flanking "swoop and counter-swoop" (as Churchill has described it) both sides were of course very much aware of the importance of eventually anchoring their flanks upon the sea. Also both sides began to realize that a decisive victory by encirclement was no longer likely. Each became very much aware

French prisoners of war in Germany. (U.S. Signal Corps)

of the defensive strength the opponent would gain when its northern flank could be anchored against the seacoast, and not subject to the fluctuations of cavalry maneuvers. As a consequence, instead of racing to the sea, as some historians have suggested, both sides were in fact trying to prolong the line as far as possible behind the other's flank to avoid reaching the sea too soon. In this way each hoped to gain room for maneuver, and to establish a position from which the enemy's line could later be breached in a successful penetration and envelopment. In addition, the Allies wished to preserve as much French and Belgian territory as possible from German occupation.

By early October, seizure of the Channel ports of Dunkirk, Calais, and Boulogne became the German objective. The Allies, for their part, hoped to be able to swing their line to the northeast far enough to link up with the Belgian defensive positions around Antwerp.

Antwerp

On August 18, in the face of the overwhelming might of the German First Army, King Albert had begun his retreat to the fortified port of Antwerp, with his field army of approximately 75,000 men. There were about 60,000 inferior troops already in the Antwerp garrison. The withdrawal was complete on August 20. Kluck had left behind a reinforced corps, totaling about 60,000 men, under General Hans von Beseler, to blockade the Belgian army, and to prevent it from interfering with the invasion and from harassing the German lines of communication. Von Beseler, of course, did not have enough troops to attempt to besiege the fortress.

On August 24, having learned of the battles which had been taking place at Mons and on the Sambre, King Albert made a sortie

71

King Albert of Belgium in his headquarters. (Imperial War Museum)

against the blockading Germans, hoping this would relieve the pressure on the British and French. He called off the attack two days later, however, upon learning of the Allied retreat. Albert led his army in another sortie on September 9, when he learned that some troops had been withdrawn from von Beseler's command to rush to the struggle then taking place along the Marne. It is doubtful if Albert's efforts had any effect whatsoever on German dispositions for that battle, but the Belgians came very close to breaking through the weakened German lines.

The Belgian sortie probably did have an effect on the Kaiser, however. On the afternoon of September 9, he issued orders that Antwerp must be captured. Thus, as Albert was planning a third sortie, on September 20, he learned that German reinforcements were arriving from the south. He canceled his planned attack, and prepared for a desperate defense.

Antwerp during the siege; a German shell burst over the Scheldt River tem-
porary bridge; note the section pulled out on the right, permitting a small boat
to enter the harbor. (U.S. War Department General Staff)

It was about this time that the Allies began to realize the strategic importance of ending the "Race to the Sea" at Antwerp. Also, they wished to sustain their gallant, and thus far neglected, Belgian allies on Belgian soil. Further, they welcomed the prospect of adding the small Belgian field army to their overextended ranks. Finally, the British were particularly anxious to prevent the Germans from obtaining a foothold on the Belgian seacoast opposite Britain.

No Allied supplies or reinforcements could get into Antwerp from the sea, because neutral Holland would not permit any military traffic up the Scheldt River, which passes through Dutch territory before reaching the sea. While the British were debating the possibility of sending troops from England, to join one of Joffre's "swoops" in a drive to Antwerp, the situation suddenly became urgent. On September 28 the German reinforcements arrived at Antwerp. They consisted of only three reserve divisions, but they were accompanied

Winston Churchill, First Lord of the British Admiralty. (U.S. Signal Corps)

by large numbers of the heavy guns which had smashed the fortifications at Liège and Namur. At once the attackers began the same
systematic fort-by-fort destruction which had overwhelmed the other
Belgian fortresses. Belgian counterattacks, attempting to reach the
guns, or to drive them out of range, were repulsed by the Germans.
Slowly, inexorably, the Germans inched closer to Antwerp from the
east and south.

There was still a narrow passageway from Antwerp to the west,
just south of the Dutch frontier, held open by Belgian troops. Albert

and the Belgian government decided that their mobile field army should withdraw to join the Allies before this escape route was blocked by the Germans. Late that night the British government was informed of the proposed evacuation. Winston Churchill, First Lord of the Admiralty, rushed from London to consult with the Belgian king. The Belgian government agreed to postpone its withdrawal order until the consultations with Churchill were concluded. On October 4, at Churchill's urgent request, a British naval brigade arrived, and immediately entered the battle. Two additional British divisions — the 7th and the 3rd Cavalry — were rushed to British ports, and were scheduled to arrive at Ostend and Zeebrugge on the sixth or the seventh. This force, under General Henry C. Rawlinson, was organized as the British IV Corps.

But the inexorable German bombardment and advance continued. On October 6 the last Belgian fort east of the Scheldt was overrun. The Belgians could delay no longer, as Churchill reluctantly agreed. That night the mobile field army — about 70,000 men — began to evacuate the city; the next morning Belgian troops joined the British troops landing on the seacoast at Ostend and Zeebrugge. The evacuation of Antwerp was completed late on October 8.

Antwerp held out for less than two more days. On October 9 German troops forced their way into the city. Next morning the last Belgian defender surrendered. The Germans pushed westward in pursuit of the retreating Belgian army. The "Race to the Sea" approached its climax.

Landing of the British 7th Division at Zeebrugge, October 7, 1914. (Imperial War Museum)

Belgian cavalry and motor trucks preparing to evacuate Antwerp, October, 1914. (Imperial War Museum)

A German infantry soldier on the Belgian coast near Antwerp after the fall of the city. (U.S. Signal Corps)

The First Battle of Ypres

Preliminaries in Flanders

During the first week of October the British Expeditionary Force was withdrawn from the Aisne front and moved to Flanders for the climactic operations in the "Race to the Sea." The British were still in somewhat better condition than most of the overextended French troops, and Joffre believed that they would have the best chance of reaching Antwerp to link up with the Belgians and with the arriving British IV Corps. Furthermore, it would simplify supply arrangements if the British could be located near the Channel ports, so that

77

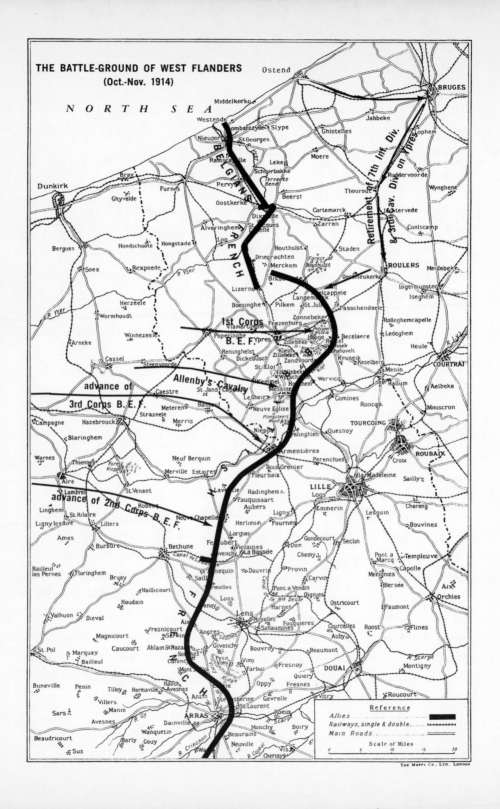

THE BATTLE-GROUND OF WEST FLANDERS
(Oct.-Nov. 1914)

NORTH SEA

Ostend

BRUGES

Middelkerke
Westende
Lombartzyde Slype
Nieuport St Georges
Ramscapelle
Leke
Moere
Ghistelles
Jabbke
Lophem
Rudderroorde
Wynghene

Dunkirk

Bray
Furnes
Ghyvelde
Pervyse
Oostkerke

Beerst
Dixmude
St Jacques
Thourout
Zarren
Cortemarck
Oostervede
Coolscamp

BELGIANS
FRENCH

Retirement of 7th Inf. Div.
& 3rd Cav. Diddervoorde on Ypres

Bergues
Hondschoote Hoogstade
Alveringhem
Loo

Soex
Rexpoede
R Yser

Staden
Lizerne
ROULERS
Meulebeke
Ingelmunster
Iseghem

Herzeele
Wormhoudt
Driegrachten
Merckem
Bixschoote

Houthulst
Forest of Houthulst
Merckem
Oostnieukerke

Boesinghe Pilkem
St Jul.
Langemarck
Passchendaele
Rolleghemcapelle

Winnezeele
Arneke
1st Corps
B.E.F.
Vlamertinghe
Frezenburg
Zonnebeke
Polygon
Wood
Becelaere
Ledeghem
Heule

Cassel
Steenvoorde
Poperinghe Ypres
Hooge
Zillebeke
Gheluvelt
Kruseik
Kezelberg
Menin

advance of
3rd Corps B.E.F.
Allenby's Cavalry
Caestre
St Jans
Reninghelst
Dickebusch
St Eloi
Klein
Zillebeke
Zandvoord
Hollebeke
Wytschaete
Kemmel Hollebeke
Wervicq
Comines
Hallum
Roncq

COURTRAI

Aelbeke
Mouscron

Meteren
Strazeele
Bailleul
Neuve Eglise
Le Gheir
Messines
Ploegsteert
Wood
Nieppe
Warneton
Quesnoy

TOURCOING
Croix
ROUBAIX

Campagne
Hazebrouck
Merris
Armentières
Bois Grenier
Perenchies
Sailly

Blaringhem
Thiennes
Forest of
Nieppe
Neuf Berquin
Estaires
Merville
Fleurbaix
La Madeleine

Warnes
Aire
Lambres
St Venant
Robecq
Lavantie
Radinghem
Fauquissart
Aubers
LILLE
Loos
Emmerin
Lesquin
Chereng
Bouvines

Lingham
St Hilaire
Neuve Chapelle
Herlies
Ligny
Fournes
Gondecourt
Seclin
Pont a
Marcq
Templeuve
Capelle

Ligny les Aire
Lillers
Ames
Burbure
Bethune
Festubert
Violaines
Givenchy La Bassée
Don
Chemy
Carvin
Provin
Menignies
Bersee
Aix
Orchies

Bailleul
les Pernes
Floringhem
Bruay
Haillicourt
Houdain
Hacquin
Sailly
Cambrin
melles
Loos
Canal
Pont a Vendin
Oignies
Harnes
Courcelles
Ostricourt
Faumont
Roost
Flines

Valhuon
Dieval
Magnicourt
Caucourt
Fresnicourt
Servins
Angres
Souchez
Ablain St Nazaire
Souchez
Petit
Vimy
Bouvry
Beaumont
Auby
DOUAI
R Scarpe
Montigny

St Pol
Marquay
Bailleul
Buneville
Penin
Tilloy
Hermaville
Mont St Eloi
Carency
Vimy
Ridge
Farbus
Fresnoy
Quiery
Oppy
Fresnes
Vitry
Roucourt

LENS
Noyelles
Sallaumines
Fouquieres

Sars
Villers
Manin
Haute
Avesnes
Anzin
St Catherine
St Laurent
Gavrelle
Roeux
R Scarp
Boiry
Monchy

Beaudricourt
Sus
R Gy
Dainville
Wanquetin
Gouy
ARRAS
Beaurains
Neuville
R Crinchon
R Cojeul
VIS
Cherisy

Reference
Allies
Railways, single & double
Main Roads
Scale of Miles
0   5   10   15   20

The Mappa Co. Ltd. London

their lines of communications would not cut across those of French troops in Flanders, Artois, and Picardy. Field Marshal Sir John French was in full agreement with Joffre, and so the British movement began.

Upon his arrival in Flanders, on October 10, Sir John was disappointed to learn of the evacuation of Antwerp. But the Belgians and General Rawlinson's IV Corps still held a substantial portion of northern Belgium. With British assistance, the Belgians had turned at Ghent and halted the German pursuit from Antwerp. The arrival of German reinforcements soon forced the Belgians to withdraw northwestward from Ghent, but Field Marshal French was confident that the continuing arrival of his own troops would more than offset this German advantage. It appeared to him and to Joffre that the Allies, despite the loss of Antwerp, had already won the "Race to the Sea." Within a week French's army would be concentrated in Flanders. Then, with Belgian assistance, Sir John expected to roll up the German right flank, recapture Lille, and drive the Germans completely out of northwestern Belgium.

On October 10 the British II Corps began to push the thin German line back from La Bassée. On October 12 and 13 the recently arrived British III Corps, under General William Pulteney, and the newly organized Cavalry Corps, under General Edmund Allenby, were assembled south of Ypres, and began to advance against growing resistance in the vicinity of the border towns of Armentières (in France) and Messines (near Ypres, in Belgium). On the fourteenth, Rawlinson's 3rd Cavalry Division established firm contact with the Cavalry Corps east of Ypres. A continuous Allied line now extended approximately to the point where the Dutch–Belgian frontier reached the North Sea. It was a tenuous line, however, dangerously strained

German troops halted by inundations in western Belgium; the mud wall in the foreground was part of a German effort to hold back the floodwaters. (U.S. War Department General Staff)

at several points by ominously increasing German pressure. Knowing that Haig's I Corps would arrive at Ypres in the next four days, and confident that the Germans had exhausted all their reserves, Sir John ordered a general advance toward Menin and Lille to begin on October 18.

Battle of the Yser

When he gave these orders, Sir John still did not fully realize that his own troops, like the Belgians and French to their north, had already been thrown back on the defensive by a new German offensive.

Unknown to the Allies, the Germans had raised five new corps of only partially trained reservists, mixed with a strong leavening of veterans, and had moved them rapidly to Flanders. Falkenhayn had shifted Prince Rupprecht's Sixth Army from the center of his line to southern Flanders, and also transferred elements of Duke Albrecht's Fourth Army to northern Flanders, where it was reconstituted to full strength with the newly raised corps. On October 12 these two German armies had begun an offensive aimed at seizing the Channel ports. Due largely to the inexperience of the new units, this German offensive was slow in gaining momentum, and so it was not until October 15 that Sir John French realized that his troops were defending instead of attacking.

Joffre had grasped the situation more quickly. He had already pulled a number of Ninth Army units out of the line, and rushed them north under the personal command of General Foch, who was to try to coordinate the operations of British, French, and Belgian troops. Foch and Field Marshal French got along very well, and in fact Foch was able to coordinate the Allied defense very effectively.

The British regulars, although hard-pressed, maintained their lines intact between La Bassée and Ypres, with the help of French reinforcements. To the north, however, the Belgians and some French units with them were thrown back to the Yser River, where they were able to halt the German advance with the help of gunfire support from British warships. When the Germans renewed the attack, however, King Albert realized that his exhausted troops could hold no longer. So he ordered the opening of canal and seawall sluice gates, inundating an area two miles wide between Dixmude and the sea. Here the Germans were unable to advance farther.

On October 19, Sir John committed Haig's I Corps to counterattack east of Ypres. By evening of the twentieth, the German offensive was completely stopped, and the initiative had passed to the

81

General Sir Douglas Haig at a railroad station in Flanders; a Belgian officer is behind him. (Imperial War Museum)

Allies. Foch and French now believed that they had so exhausted the Germans that they could go ahead with the original plan to roll up the German right flank.

The Allies again completely underestimated their opponents. In addition, heavy rains turned the low-lying Flanders countryside into a marsh. The Germans, in defensive positions on high ground east of Ypres, had little trouble in halting the Allied attacks with heavy losses, while they continued their pressure against the Belgians on the lower Yser. On October 28, Foch called off the offensive.

The Struggle for Ypres

Falkenhayn, meanwhile, had been steadily building up the strength of his Fourth and Sixth Armies. By concentrating most of five newly arrived divisions on the right wing of the Sixth Army, opposite Ypres, he had achieved a German superiority of at least six to one in the immediate vicinity of Ypres. On October 29 the Germans launched their renewed offensive. This time Falkenhayn was certain that he would break through to Calais and Boulogne.

For three days the Germans advanced slowly but steadily, greatly assisted by their substantial superiority in medium and heavy artillery. Foch and Sir John rushed French and British units from other parts of the line in a vain effort to stem the tide. On October 31, for a few hours, the Germans actually ruptured the Allied line southeast of Ypres, but magnificent tenacity on the part of the British, and splendid cooperation between the intermingled British and French units as they launched desperate counterattacks, finally closed the gap. The German advance was halted by nightfall.

After a brief pause, the Germans redoubled their efforts. They were able to put fresh troops into the battle by bringing down three divisions from the line opposite the Belgians. Despite fearful losses, they made slight gains on November 7, 8, and 9. On November 10 they renewed their attacks along the entire line, and by dawn of the eleventh had captured Dixmude from the Belgians.

At Ypres, after initial success against the exhausted and outnumbered British on November 11, the German assault was finally halted, then hurled back. This was the climax of the battle. Snow began to fall on the twelfth, making offensive operations difficult. Although the German attacks continued for twelve more days, they were un-

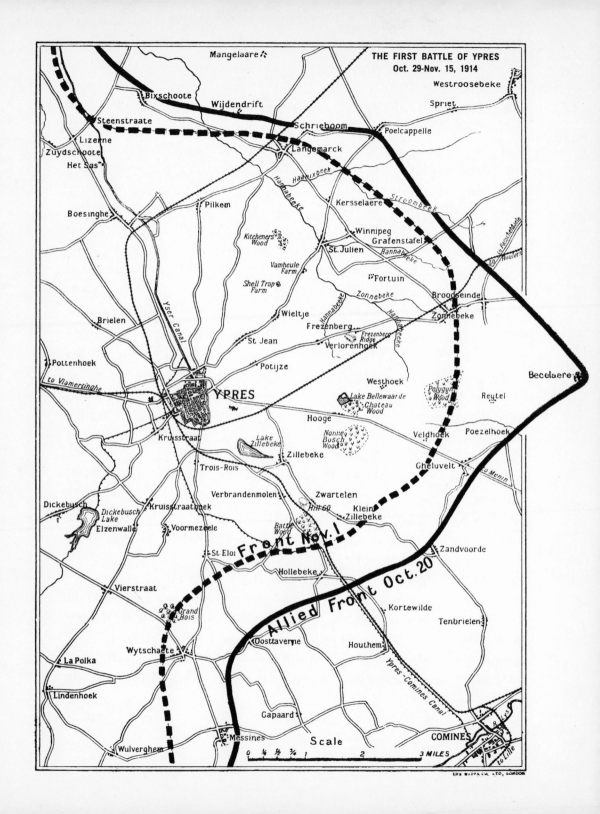

successful. The British Expeditionary Force, outnumbered nearly three to one, had held Ypres, and had stopped the Germans.

The British success at Ypres was due to a number of factors. Most important was the superiority of the training and marksmanship of the British regulars, who made up most of the BEF at the outset of the battle. Next in importance was the tough, stolid, and grim determination with which the British troops stood their ground. It was this quality which enabled the Allied leaders, and particularly Sir John French, General Haig, and General Allenby, to make the best possible use of their meager reserves. Certainly the cooperation and support of Foch and his French troops also played an important part.

When the battle was over, the BEF was practically destroyed as a fighting force. Half of the regulars — officers and men — were dead or wounded. But in the process they had smashed the German Fourth Army, inflicting perhaps twice as many casualties as they had suffered. After Ypres the British regulars were largely replaced by Territorial militia soldiers, by volunteers, and — later — by conscripts.

The Kaiser, who had arrived at the front in early October to witness the expected triumphal advance of his armies to the Channel, was given reason to regret his earlier remarks about Britain's "contemptible little army." At Ypres — or "Wipers" as the British Tommy called it — "the Old Contemptibles" had their finest hour.

Closing Weeks of 1914

With the end of the Battle of Ypres, open warfare completely ceased on the Western Front. Two lines of entrenchments faced each other from the Swiss Alps to the North Sea. Both sides began to improve their defenses by digging more and deeper trenches (except in the

85

Flanders lowlands, where the troops struck water about a foot below the surface). Barbed-wire entanglements began to appear in front of the trench parapets, so placed that attackers would be halted in front of carefully constructed machine-gun positions. Behind the trenches were lines of rapid-firing artillery pieces. The Germans — who had suffered at the hands of the light French 75-mm gun in the open fighting at the Marne — hastily built up their own light artillery. The Allies, who discovered the need for heavier, longer-ranged, and higher-trajectory weapons when they were halted at the Aisne, now hastened to produce medium and heavy artillery.

In general, the Germans had selected better positions, and had prepared them more effectively. But trenches, barbed wire, machine guns, and artillery shells are great equalizers. A complete stalemate had been reached on the Western Front. For three years both sides tried to figure out ways of breaking this stalemate, while simultaneously improving their positions to make them nearly impregnable, thus still further compounding the problem.

Strangely, despite the events of September, October, and November, neither side yet fully realized the fundamental stability of the stalemate. Joffre believed that after a rest, and with adequate preparation, the Allies could still break through. He knew that in late November and early December the Germans had sent several corps to the East Front, and he knew that his troops now outnumbered the Germans in the West. He issued orders for a new offensive, to extend along the entire line, from the sea to Verdun.

The Allied offensive began on December 14. It was a catastrophe. For ten red days the Allies beat in vain against the rapidly growing German net of field fortifications. By December 24 the offensive had ended, except in Champagne, where a few slight gains had encouraged Joffre's hope that a breakthrough could still be made. At the end of the year, French divisions were still smashing themselves to bits against the German defenses in this First Battle of Champagne.

After less than five months of fighting, Allied troops in the West had suffered almost exactly 1,000,000 casualties. More than 80 per cent of these were French; the remainder were shared between the British and the Belgians. German losses were perhaps slightly less, but were probably more than 900,000 killed, wounded, and captured. Never before nor since have opposing armies suffered such tremendous losses in such a brief span of time.

Damage to the Cloth Hall and nearby houses in Ypres, during the first German bombardment of the city, October, 1914. (Imperial War Museum)

Index

89